Parables from The Fishin' Hole

Study Notes by
Mary Guenther

Participant's Guide

Published by

Nelson
multi media group
A THOMAS NELSON COMPANY

A division of Thomas Nelson Publishers

Copyright © 2001 by Thomas Nelson Publishers

All rights reserved.

No part of this book may be reproduced, stored in a retrieval system, or transmitted in any form or by any means, electronic, mechanical, photocopying, recording, or otherwise, without the written permission of Thomas Nelson Publishers.

Scripture quotations are from The Holy Bible, New King James Version, Copyright © 1979, 1980, 1982, Thomas Nelson, Inc., Publishers.

The video elements of this material are in the public domain. The use of the characters from the video throughout does not signify the endorsement of the characters or actors of this or any other product.

Printed in the United States of America
ISBN 0-8499-8960-4

For Information
Call Thomas Nelson Publishers 1-800-251-4000

Table of Contents

	Page
Session One Dogs, Dogs, Dogs	1
Session Two Andy Discovers America	13
Session Three Class Reunion	25
Session Four Andy's English Valet	35

About the Author

Mary Guenther is a freelance writer living in Nashville, Tennessee. She contributed the character sketches for *The Women of Faith Study Bible,* and co-authored *The Bedtime Bible* for children. In her former position as manager of book publishing for Promise Keepers, she was responsible for numerous publications, including the men's video retreat kit, *Face to Face, An Encounter with Christ.* She has written and edited numerous EZ Lesson Plans for Thomas Nelson Multimedia.

Parables from The Fishin' Hole

Session One
Dogs, Dogs, Dogs

Dogs, Dogs, Dogs
(Mercy Is As Mercy Does)

LUKE 10:27
You shall love the LORD your God with all your heart, with all your soul, with all your strength, and with all your mind, and your neighbor as yourself.

Her tiny, frail figure took center stage in the 20th Century. Yet, no one who knew her in her younger years saw Mother Teresa as one who was in any way remarkable. She was average—average in looks, average in intelligence, energy, and personality. But she had an extraordinary passion for the unloved and unlovely, the poorest of the poor. She poured out her energies on the homeless of Calcutta without thought of reward, recognition, or thanks. The depth of her mercy stunned the whole world.

We all need mercy. And the truth is, we'd all like to be merciful. Yet we often fail to respond to others in need. Why is that?

Dogs, Dogs, Dogs is, of course, about dogs. But it doesn't take much imagination to see how its principles could also apply to people and the ways we talk ourselves out of caring for them.

How would you define the word "mercy"?

_____
_____
_____
_____

> Live so that when your children think of fairness, caring, and integrity, they think of you.[1]

Assuredly, I say to you, whoever does not receive the kingdom of God as a little child will by no means enter it."

Mark 10:15

"Caught" More than Taught?

Opie was a lucky boy. He had a good example in Andy. Thoughtfulness and generosity were high values in their home.

What things did Andy do in the beginning of the episode to model mercy for Opie?
_____
_____

What made Barney and Andy change their attitude toward the dogs?
_____
_____

Have you ever begun a work of mercy, then given up when it began to take more time and energy?
❑ Yes ❑ No ❑ Often

If so, discuss what other options you might have had in that situation.
_____
_____

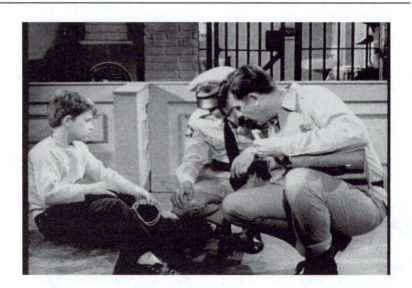

Children Can Lead, Too

Trevor Ferrell was a normal 11-year-old in suburban Philadelphia. He loved video games and motorbikes, got average grades in school, and fought with his brother and sisters from time to time. But one winter night, Trevor was riveted by a spot on the late night news — homeless people bedding down on hard, cold sidewalks without any warm cover. Surely, this couldn't happen in Philadelphia!

Please do not duplicate.

Trevor begged his parents to take him downtown right away. He wanted to give someone a blanket, a sandwich, and his own pillow. At first, his parents protested—it was late and it might be dangerous.

But finally, they did what he asked. From that one encounter, Trevor went on to spearhead a nationally recognized ministry to the homeless of Philadelphia. His infectious love for the poor more than compensated for his lack of experience and political savvy as a child. "Trevor's Place" still ministers in downtown Philadelphia today, almost 30 years later.

What if the Ferrels had talked Trevor out of his impulse? Happily, the whole family joined him instead.

Why is it sometimes easier for a child to respond mercifully to a situation than an adult?

_____

_____

Has God ever used a child to lead you to respond in mercy?
❑ Yes ❑ No ❑ Often

If so, did you follow his/her lead?

_____

_____

Let's Get Practical

Opie thought about the dogs, while Andy and Barney began to think more about the Courthouse image.

> The quality of mercy is not strain'd,
> It droppeth as the gentle rain from heaven.
>
> --William Shakespeare

He has shown you, O man, what is good; and what does the LORD require of you but to do justly, to love mercy, and to walk humbly with your God?

Micah 6:8

So, both Andy and Barney try to convince Opie that he is overreacting to the dogs' situation. Let's catch their conversation.

Barney:
I said to myself, "If I was a dog, where would I want to go? I'd want to be out in the open, out in the wide open spaces where I could run and play.
Opie: You just left all them dogs out in the middle of nowhere?
Andy: I wouldn't worry about the dogs. They'll be fine.
Opie: I sure hope so.
Opie: Pa, them dogs, they're out there. They're out in an open field, Pa. I'm worried about them, Pa.
Andy: You needn't be. They'll be okay.

What do you think Andy was trying to do?

_____
_____
_____

What negative effect could this approach have on a child's natural response to someone in need?

_____
_____
_____

Have you ever tried to talk someone out of their urge to help someone else by saying there was no need for concern?
❏ Yes   ❏ No   ❏ Often

If so, what was the result?

_____
_____
_____

When Opie still worried, Barney applied adult logic.

Barney: Opie, you don't need to worry about 'em. What can happen to 'em?
Opie: Well, that lightning. What about that?
Barney: A dog can't get struck by lightning. You know why? Because he's too close to the ground. See, lightning strikes tall things…Now, if they was giraffes out there in that field, then we'd be in trouble. But you sure don't have to worry about dogs.
Opie: I'm worried about 'em, Pa.
Barney: Aaw, look, Opie. What were dogs a million years ago? Wild animals, right? Wolves, coyotes, they know how to hunt and fish and look for shelter. Take those two big Airedales. They look healthy as horses. And that little spotted one? Why he was in fine shape!
Opie: But the little one I first come in with—he was a trembler, wasn't he?
Barney: Well, the big ones will look after him. Dogs take care of their own.

What happens when Opie still seems unconvinced?

_____
_____
_____

When Opie grew silent and just looked big-eyed at Barney, Barney unloaded *all* of his vast knowledge of dogs and their behavior.

Barney: And you know dogs have a way of keeping dry. They're insulated you see. They got fur and that keeps 'em cool in the summer and warm and dry in the winter. They're really set up a lot better'n human beings, as far as that goes.
Opie: (silence)
Barney: As far as the little one goes, the big ones'll take care of him, the little trembly one.

"Boy, giraffes are selfish. Just running around looking out for number one, getting hit by lightning…"

--Barney Fife

> "You did a good thing, Barn. You did a cardinal act of mercy."
>
> --Andy Taylor

> And they're short, you see. Close to the ground. They can't get struck by lightning. Now if they was giraffes, they'd a been hit by now. But dogs are short and they take care of their own. Giraffes don't. . .

Barnie was talking about dogs, but his arguments sound familiar. Just for fun, place the name of some group, family or person in the following blanks to see if Barney's reasoning could apply.

- _____ always managed to get by in the past without help.

- _____ have a way of keeping dry (keeping warm/keeping cool).

- _____ are well set up for their circumstances.

- _____ take care of their own.

Now put <u>your own name</u> in the blanks:

- _____ always managed to get by in the past without help.

- _____ has a way of keeping dry (keeping warm/keeping cool).

- _____ is well set up for his/her circumstances.

How might you feel if someone responded to your needs in this way?

_____
_____
_____
_____
_____

Please do not duplicate.

Mercy for the Merciful

2 CORINTHIANS 9:6
But this I say: He who sows sparingly will also reap sparingly, and he who sows bountifully will also reap bountifully.

Scripture says that mercy often inspires mercy in return. How was this principle demonstrated in this episode?

_____

_____

_____

Have you ever experienced something like this in your own life? If so, share your story.

_____

_____

_____

A little girl was late arriving home from school, so her mother scolded:
"Why are you so late?"
"I had to help another girl. She was in trouble."
"What did you do to help her?"
"Oh, I sat down and helped her cry."

— Anonymous

Blessed are the merciful, for they shall obtain mercy.

Matthew 5:7

MERCY LITMUS TEST

Read aloud and briefly discuss each quote below. Check the appropriate box, noting how each applies to your own personal life experience.

I expect to pass through life but once. If, therefore, there be any kindness I can show, or any good thing I can do to any fellow being, let me do it now, for I shall not pass this way again.   – William Penn
❏ Applies   ❏ Sometimes Applies   ❏ Does Not Apply

Don't forget that we are ultimately judged by what we give, not by what we get.[2]
❏ Applies   ❏ Sometimes Applies   ❏ Does Not Apply

When a child wants to tell you something, look them in the eyes and give them your full attention.[3]
❏ Applies   ❏ Sometimes Applies   ❏ Does Not Apply

Remember that everyone you meet is looking for affirmation, direction, and hope.[4]
❏ Applies   ❏ Sometimes Applies   ❏ Does Not Apply

Don't be surprised if your happiest moments are when you are doing things for others.[5]
❏ Applies   ❏ Sometimes Applies   ❏ Does Not Apply

Live so that when your children think of fairness, caring, and integrity, they think of you.[6]
❏ Applies   ❏ Sometimes Applies   ❏ Does Not Apply

1. **Which of the above quotes is closest to your own idea of mercy? Why?**
   _____
   _____
   _____
   _____

2. **Which presents the greatest challenge to you? Why?**
   _____
   _____
   _____
   _____

Please do not duplicate.

Personal Notes

Personal Notes

[1] H. Jackson Brown, Jr., *Life's Instructions for Wisdom, Success, and Happiness* (Nashville: Rutledge Hill Press, 2000)
[2] Ibid
[3] Ibid
[4] Ibid
[5] Ibid
[6] Ibid

Parables from The Fishin' Hole

Session Two
Andy Discovers America

Andy Discovers America
(Words RULE!)

JAMES 3:3-5
Indeed, we put bits in horses' mouths that they may obey us, and we turn their whole body. Look also at ships: although they are so large and are driven by fierce winds, they are turned by a very small rudder wherever the pilot desires. Even so the tongue is a little member and boasts great things. See how great a forest a little fire kindles!

Words have *power*. You may remember that in the musical, *My Fair Lady,* Henry Higgins wagered that he could turn a grubby street merchant into an aristocratic lady, merely by teaching her to speak proper English. Of course, he won his bet and Eliza Dolittle wowed his snobbish set with her perfect English (stunning wardrobe aside).

Okay, so *My Fair Lady* is fiction. But in real life, our words have power, too. In the above scripture, James says that the tongue (our words) is like a rudder. That one little part determines the direction of the whole ship. Think for a minute about how your words affected your family today. Multiply that by 365 days a year for many years and you can see how important it is to be sure that your words have the kind of impact that you want them to have!

As a group, list some of the positive ways we can use words:

_____   _____
_____   _____
_____   _____
_____   _____
_____   _____

> If you wish to know the mind of a man, listen to his words.[1]

> Man's mind once stretched by a new idea, never regains its original dimension.
>
> --Oliver Wendell Holmes

Now list some of the negative ways:

_____   _____
_____   _____
_____   _____
_____   _____

Getting Off Course is Easy!

Andy Discovers America gives us a picture of how words can go awry, but also how they can turn a near-disaster around.

It all begins one morning, with a typical father-son exchange over breakfast. As we see, what Andy *said* is not necessarily what Opie *heard*.

Andy said: You see, Op, you're not the only one who has trouble with history. History was hard for me, too. It is for some people. So, you just do the best you can, grow up to be a fine young fella, and I'll be satisfied . . .And if you don't know the answer, you just tell Miss What's-Her-Name that you come by it naturally.

Andy means to affirm Opie, as any parent would. But his casual response to Opie's situation stirs up a firestorm.

Opie heard: (When asked why he didn't do his homework)
Well, my Pa said it wasn't too important, all that stuff. He said he never had to learn it, so why should I?
Miss Krump: Opie, your father told you not to do your homework?
Opie: He said it wasn't my fault. It's hard for everybody.

What common communication mistakes did Andy make that morning?
_____
_____
_____

Why do you think Miss Krump was so angry at Andy?
_____
_____
_____

What mistakes did she make in confronting Andy?
_____
_____
_____

Have you ever reacted to a situation after getting only one person's version of what happened?
❑ Yes ❑ No ❑ Often

If so, what was the result?
_____
_____
_____

> Among the graffiti on a subway wall:
>
> "This life is a test. It is only a test. Had this been an actual life you would have received instructions as to what to do and where to go."[2]

"You see that foot? How could that great big foot—all of if—fit in my mouth?"

--Andy Taylor

Getting Back on Course Takes Humility!

2 Timothy 2:24-25
And a servant of the Lord must not quarrel but be gentle to all, able to teach, patient, in humility correcting those who are in opposition, if God perhaps will grant them repentance, so that they may know the truth.

Realizing his gaff, Andy is quick to assume responsibility for his mistake. That's an important first step! Then he uses his understanding of young boys to help them accept the course correction they need to make.

Andy: Maybe they won't be able to find you another teacher, after all the trouble you give Miss Krump. . .
I'm glad for you! You're lucky, you know that. You know what you should do? You should go out and celebrate! Go out and play and have a good time.
Now you won't have to learn all that dull stuff about all them Indians and Redcoats and muskets and stuff. . .

Why did Andy's approach work so well?
_____
_____
_____
_____

On the other hand, Miss Krump was headed for a sand bar when she tried to influence the boys in her class to study history.

Please do not duplicate.

> **Miss Krump**: *[Thoughtfully]*
> Boys, every morning when we come in this class, we say a pledge of allegiance to the flag. I just wonder if any of you boys ever hear those words or if you ever think about what they mean. I doubt it.
> *[Then with growing anger]*
> Do any of you have the faintest idea about how this country got started or have any interest in learning about it? If you have, you haven't shown it . . . .

What got in the way of Miss Krump's appeal to the boys?
_____
_____
_____

What could she have done to avoid this?
_____
_____
_____

> There is no better test for a man's ultimate integrity than his behavior when he is wrong.[3]

Bringing the Ship into Harbor

COLOSSIANS 3:12B-13
Put on tender mercies, kindness, humility, meekness, longsuffering; bearing with one another, and forgiving one another, if anyone has a complaint against another; even as Christ forgave you, so you also must do.

This time, Miss Krump humbled herself. She recognized her own part in the misunderstanding with Andy and took action to repair her earlier angry outburst. Her *words* healed the rift.

> A child is a person who is going to carry on what you have started . . . the fate of humanity is in his hands.
>
> --Abraham Lincoln

Miss Krump: (to Andy) What did you do to those boys?
Andy: Nothing.
Miss Krump: You must have done something.
Andy: They come by and we had a little talk.

To what did Andy attribute his success with the boys?

_____
_____
_____

What would have happened if Miss Krump hadn't gone to repair things with Andy?

_____
_____
_____

Looking back on the whole situation, Andy and Miss Krump finally agree.

Andy: I reckon you do have to be careful what you say around young'uns.
Miss Krump: They do try to turn things to their own advantage.

Words have power. You might even say, words *rule!*

Please do not duplicate.
20

> There's no place like home. There's no place like home.
>
> --Dorothy
> *(The Wizard of Oz)*

But the myth prevails, and we see Andy and Barney begin this episode reminiscing about their childhood and high school years.

> **Andy:** What're you saving this rock for? Is it worth anything?
> **Barney:** Well, not monetarily, but it has a lot of sentimental value. That was my daddy's rock. There's a lot of happiness connected with that rock. It used to sit on my daddy's desk. I used it to strike kitchen matches on it and hold them to my daddy's pipe. You know, for a little fella it was a big kick to strike a match and hold it to your daddy's pipe.

What made lighting a match so memorable to both men?

_____

_____

_____

What's your favorite memory from your childhood.

_____

_____

_____

How would you describe your childhood:
❑ Happy   ❑ Sad   ❑ Neutral

Why?

_____

_____

_____

Please do not duplicate.

LITMUS TEST ON SPEECH

Read aloud and briefly discuss the following quotes. Check the appropriate box for each quote as it applies to your own life experience.

Man is the only kind of varmit that sets his own trap, baits it, then steps in it. --John Steinbeck, *Sweet Thursday*[4]
❏ Applies ❏ Sometimes Applies ❏ Does not apply

Life is a public performance on the violin, in which you must learn the instrument as you go along. –E. M. Forester[5]
❏ Applies ❏ Sometimes Applies ❏ Does not apply

Few slanders can stand the wear of silence. – Mark Twain
❏ Applies ❏ Sometimes Applies ❏ Does not apply

Folks who think they must always speak the truth overlook another good choice—silence. --C. L. Null
❏ Applies ❏ Sometimes Applies ❏ Does not apply

When ideas fail, words come in very handy. –Goethe
❏ Applies ❏ Sometimes Applies ❏ Does not apply

The difference between the right word and the almost right word is the difference between lightning and the lightning bug. –Mark Twain
❏ Applies ❏ Sometimes Applies ❏ Does not apply

1. **Which of the above quotes is closest to your own use of words? Why?**
   _____
   _____
   _____
   _____

2. **Which presents the greatest challenge to you? Why?**
   _____
   _____
   _____
   _____

Talk about power!

MY MOTHER TAUGHT ME
My Mother taught me LOGIC . . . If you fall off that swing and break your neck, you can't go to the store with me.
My Mother taught me MEDICINE . . . If you don't stop crossing your eyes, they're going to freeze that way.
My Mother taught me TO THINK AHEAD . . . If you don't pass your spelling test, you'll never get a good job!
My Mother taught me ESP . . . Put your sweater on; don't you think that I know when you're cold?
My Mother taught me TO MEET A CHALLENGE . . . What were you thinking? Answer me when I talk to you... Don't talk back to me!
My Mother taught me HUMOR . . . When that lawn mower cuts off your toes, don't come running to me.
My Mother taught me how to BECOME AN ADULT . . . If you don't eat your vegetables, you'll never grow up.
My Mother taught me about GENETICS . . . You are just like your father!
My Mother taught me about my ROOTS . . . Do you think you were born in a barn?
My Mother taught me about the WISDOM of AGE . . . When you get to be my age, you will understand.
My Mother taught me about ANTICIPATION . . . Just wait until your father gets home.
My Mother taught me about RECEIVING . . . You are going to get it when we get home.
And my all time favorite thing-JUSTICE . . . one day you will have kids, and I hope they turn out just like YOU . . . then you'll see what it's like.

Moms Are Special[6]

Ad-libs work, too!

A first grade teacher collected old, well-known proverbs. She gave each child in her class the first half of a proverb, and asked them to come up with the rest. Here are some choice replies.

- Ambition is a poor excuse for . . . not having enough sense to be lazy.
- As you shall make your bed so . . . shall you mess it up.
- Better be safe than . . . punch a 5th grader.
- Strike while the . . . bug is close.
- Its always darkest before . . . daylight savings time
- You can lead a horse to water but . . . how?
- Don't bite the hand that . . . looks dirty.
- A miss is as good as a . . . Mr.
- You can't teach an old dog new . . . math.
- It you lie down with the dogs . . . you'll stink in the morning.
- The pen is mightier than the . . . pigs
- An idle mind is . . . the best way to relax.
- Where there's smoke, there's . . . pollution.
- Happy the bride who . . . gets all the presents.
- A penny saved is . . . not much.
- Two's company, three's . . . the musketeers.
- Laugh and the whole world laughs with you, cry and . . . you have to blow your nose.
- Children should be seen and not . . . spanked or grounded.
- When the blind leadeth the blind . . . get out of the way.[7]

Personal Notes

Personal Notes

[1] Herbert V. Prochnow, *Speaker's & Toastmaster's Handbook,* (Rocklin, CA: Primas Publishing, 1993)
[2] Lowell D. Streiker, *Nelson's big Book of Laughter* (Nashville: Thomas Nelson, 2000)
[3] Herbert V. Prochnow, *Speaker's & Toastmaster's Handbook* (Rocklin, CA: Primas Publishing, 1993)
[4] Lowell D. Streiker, *Nelson's big Book of Laughter* (Nashville: Thomas Nelson, 2000)
[5] Ibid
[6] Ibid
[7] Ibid

Please do not duplicate.

Parables from The Fishin' Hole

Session Three
Class Reunion

Class Reunion
(Contentment Is An Inside Job)

ACTS 17:26
And He has made from one blood every nation of men to dwell on all the face of the earth, and has determined their preappointed times and the boundaries of their dwellings.

We've all heard the adage, "Money can't buy happiness." But if we're honest, something inside us doubts that (unless we are rich). And what about, "Significance doesn't come from success"? That too is hard to believe (unless we are highly successful). You could go on—youth, beauty, intelligence, a slim body, power, fame, learning. All are high values in our culture, but none guarantee contentment and well being. So, where is contentment and how do we get there?

In *Class Reunion*, Andy explores some options and finds the answer where he may never have thought to look.

How would you define the word "contentment"?

_____

_____

_____

Now godliness with contentment is great gain. For we brought nothing into this world, and it is certain we can carry nothing out. And having food and clothing, with these we shall be content.

1 Timothy 6:6-8

Contentment In The Past

Ah, the good old days. Whether they were the 50s, the 60s, the 70s, or the 90s, our childhood years stand out as the high water mark. We remember the happy times and gloss over the bad. Somehow, the sun was always shining and every meal ended with our favorite dessert. *Right.*

Contentment In The Present

ECCLESIASTES 3:12-13
I know that nothing is better for them than to rejoice, and to do good in their lives, and also that every man should eat and drink and enjoy the good of all his labor--it is the gift of God.

At the class reunion, Andy and Barney find the relationships from high school years are not really as tight as they remembered.

> **Ramona**: You are just the man I've been looking for. Would you give us two glasses of punch, bartender?
> **Andy**: This is Barney Fife.
> **Ramona**: Oh. Delighted to meet you, Mr. Fife.
> **Barney**: Oh, come off it, Ramona.
> **Ramona**: I beg your pardon?
> **Barney**: Barney. Barney Fife. Social studies 1-A. "Tweeky".
> **Ramona**: I'm sorry. I...I...I'm trying to place you, but I'm afraid I can't.
> **Hubby**: It has been a long time, Mr. Fife.
> **Barney**: What do you know about it?
> **Andy**: Easy, Barn.
> **Hubby**: (to Ramona) Why don't we dance, honey?
> **Barney**: The tears on my pillow bespeak the pain in my heart!
> **Andy**: She's coverin' up, Barn. She's fightin' it.

How would you describe your high school years?
❏ Happy   ❏ Miserable   ❏ Neutral

Briefly, share one experience from high school that demonstrates your answer above.

_____

_____

_____

Enjoy the little things, for one day you may look back and realize they were the big things.

—Robert Brault[1]

So teach us to number our days, that we may gain a heart of wisdom.

Psalm 90:12

Do past relationships seem better than your present ones? Why or why not?

_____
_____
_____

How does that affect your current state of contentment?

_____
_____
_____

Contentment In The Future

Andy flirts with memories and a relationship from the past as the basis for happiness in the future. He learns an important lesson in the process.

Andy to Sharon: Can you stay awhile.
Sharon: I'd love to, Andy, but I can't.
Andy: Why not? Mayberry's mighty nice this time of year.
Sharon: I just can't, really. I've gotta get back to Chicago.
Andy: Why: what's so special about Chicago?
Sharon: There's my work. . .
Andy: Well, there's a lot needs doin' here.
Sharon: I know. I enjoyed growing up here. . .
Andy: Oh, it's a mighty nice place. A lot of friends. . .
Sharon: I know, but you can't live up to your potential here. In a big city, you have room to grow and expand. You can live a different kind of life.
Andy: Huh? How can life be much different if you're happy? That's the main thing, ain't it? I mean, that's the goal for every individual as a person to shoot for, ain't it? It's kind of like the prize of the game—to be happy.

Please do not duplicate.

Sharon: Yes. How do you find that here? I like to be a big fish in a big pond, not a big fish in a little pond.
Andy: What's wrong with that?
Sharon: Well, what's wrong is I don't care for that.
Andy: I do. I really do. I've found what I want.
Sharon: How do you know? You've never tried anything else.
Andy I don't have to. Even if I did try, I'd find I already found it.
PAUSE
You know something? It's comin' back to me, why you and me never got together. It's 'cause of what we're talking about right now—your wantin' to go your way, my wantin' to go my way. You reckon?
Sharon: I reckon.
Andy: How about a couple of old friends having the last dance?

In your opinion, who is right and who is wrong in the above discussion?

_____
_____
_____

A person rarely finds future happiness by reliving events from the past. Why is this so?

_____
_____
_____

As Andy realizes he is already happy, he is thankful for his life in Mayberry.

Do you thank God for the blessings in your own life, or are you stuck on what you are missing?

_____
_____
_____

> Most people are about as happy as they make up their minds to be.
>
> --Abraham Lincoln

Contentment Litmus Test

Read aloud and briefly discuss the following quotes. Check the appropriate box for each quote as it applies to your own life experience.

Happiness sneaks in through a door you didn't know you left open. —John Barrymore[2]
❏ Applies ❏ Sometimes Applies ❏ Does Not Apply

Happiness is not a goal; it is a by-product. —Eleanor Roosevelt[3]
❏ Applies ❏ Sometimes Applies ❏ Does Not Apply

It is not easy to find happiness in ourselves, and it is not possible to find it elsewhere. —Agnes Repplier[4]
❏ Applies ❏ Sometimes Applies ❏ Does Not Apply

In order to be utterly happy the only thing necessary is to refrain from comparing this moment with other moments in the past, which I often did not fully enjoy because I was comparing them with other moments of the future.
—Andre Gide[5]
❏ Applies ❏ Sometimes Applies ❏ Does Not Apply

When I don't have anything to worry about, I begin to worry about that. —Walter Kelly
❏ Applies ❏ Sometimes Applies ❏ Does Not Apply

Don't let what you cannot do interfere with what you can do. —John Wooden[6]
❏ Applies ❏ Sometimes Applies ❏ Does Not Apply

1. Which of the above quotes is closest to your own idea of contentment? Why?

2. Which presents the greatest challenge to you? Why?

3. Take a few moments to look over your answers to the questions in this study. Would you say you were basically content with your life in the past? What about the present? Why or why not?

4. Can you think of any ways to increase your sense of contentment currently, based on what we have discussed in this lesson?

Please do not duplicate.

Personal Notes

Personal Notes

---

[1] John Cook, *Positive, Motivational, Life-Affirming & Inspirational Quotations* (Newington, CT, Rubicon Press, Inc., 1994)
[2] Ibid
[3] Ibid
[4] Ibid
[5] Ibid
[6] H. Jackson Brown, Jr., *A Father's Book of Wisdom* (Nashville, Rutledge Hill Press, 1988)

Parables from The Fishin' Hole

Session Four
Andy's English Valet

Andy's English Valet
(Love That Isn't Gift-Wrapped)

ROMANS 12:10
Be kindly affectionate to one another with brotherly love, in honor giving preference to one another.

How would you define the word "acceptance"?

_____
_____
_____

> The art of acceptance is the art of making someone who has just done you a small favor wish that he might have done you a greater one.
>
> --Russell Lynes[1]

Malcolm Merriweather is different, no doubt about it. Barney's trained ear picks that right up and, as usual, Barney jumps to his own conclusion.

> **Barney**: Notice anything about this bird?
> **Andy**: Like what?
> **Barney**: Like they way he talks.
> **Andy**: What do you mean?
> **Barney**: I don't think he's from around here. Fact is, I'd say he's from somewheres else. He's a troublemaker from another country.
> **Andy**: Think so?
> **Barney**: He's a foreigner all right.

Why do you think Barney branded Malcolm a "troublemaker"?

_____
_____
_____

> No one has ever loved anyone the way everyone wants to be loved.[2]
>
> —Mignon McLaughlin

Have you ever made a snap judgment based on someone's looks or speech? (Who hasn't?)

_____
_____
_____

When you got to know that person, did your opinion change?

_____
_____
_____

> **Opie**: You sure don't sound like you're from around here.
> **Malcolm**: I'm not, I'm from Eckmond-White, England.
> **Opie**: Oh, you come from the old country, where they have all those castles and moats 'n stuff.

Why do you think Opie was so natural with Malcolm?

_____
_____
_____

Andy is pleased at first to have help around the house, but becomes unsettled when Malcolm does things differently than Aunt Bee—or anyone else he has ever known!..

> **Andy**: [indignant] No sir! I can put on my own pants!
> **Malcolm**: But the colonel . . .
> **Andy**: Never mind the colonel. Give me my pants!
> **Andy**: Let's get this straight. I can drive myself.
> **Malcolm**: Yes, sir.

Andy: I appreciate your help, but this is altogether unnecessary.
Malcolm: Yes, sir.

Why do you think Andy was so indignant about Malcolm's attention?

_____
_____
_____

Do you have similar problems when someone makes a fuss over you? If so, do you know why?

_____
_____
_____

As Malcolm grows more comfortable with Opie, he shares his heart, within Andy's earshot.

Opie: Sure is nice having you here, Mr. Malcolm.
Malcolm: It's been the nicest part of my holiday and I'm very grateful to you and your dad.
Opie: How come?
Malcolm: Well, just think. I could have traveled the length and breadth of America without ever finding out what Americans were really like. I used to think you were quite different, you know. Then I came into your house and saw how you lived. You're not different at all, really. If it hadn't been for your dad, none of this would have been possible. Looking after you and your dad has made me very, very happy.

Yet, when Barney comes to visit, Andy still seems to consider Malcolm a problem.

> Because you're not what I would have you be, I blind myself to who, in truth, you are.
>
> —Madeline L'Engle[3]

So in everything, do to others what you would have them do to you, for this sums up the Law and the Prophets.

Matthew 7:12

Barney: I Agree with you, Andy. Malcolm's just about as nice a guy as you could meet. But I still think you ought to come out and tell him.
Andy: Oh, I'll think of something . . .
Barney: It's either that or you'll have to spend the rest of the week putting up with all kinds of nonsense. It sounds to me like the guy is making a grade-A pest of himself. Why don't you tell him to forget the whole deal and be on his way?
Andy: This is one of those things where you have to wait for the right moment. If the right one ever comes, I'll try to figure out some way to tell him.

Why do you think Malcolm was so insistent to take care of Andy the way he did?

_____
_____
_____

Have you ever hurt someone else's feeling because you rejected their kindness? If so, how did that affect your relationship with that person?

_____
_____
_____

What do you think caused Andy to go after Malcolm and bring him back?

_____
_____
_____

What does the following statement mean to you:

Sometimes you best serve another person by allowing them to *serve you.*

There are no unimportant jobs, no unimportant people, no unimportant acts of kindness.[4]

Acceptance Litmus test

Read aloud and briefly discuss the following quotes. Check the appropriate box for each quote as it applies to your own life experience.

Too many of us become enraged because we have to bear the shortcomings of others. We should remember that not one of us is perfect, and that others see our defects as obviously as we see theirs. We forget too often to look at ourselves through the eyes of our friends. Let us, therefore, bear the shortcomings of each other for the ultimate benefit of everyone.
—Abraham Lincoln[5]

❏ Applies   ❏ Sometimes Applies   ❏ Does Not Apply

A man should never be ashamed to own he has been in the wrong, which is but saying in other words, that he is wiser today than he was yesterday.
—Alexander Pope[6]

❏ Applies   ❏ Sometimes Applies   ❏ Does Not Apply

It is easier to love humanity as a whole than to love one's neighbor.
—Eric Hoffer[7]

The test of courage comes when we are in the minority; the test of tolerance comes when we are in the majority.
—Ralph W. Sockman[8]

❏ Applies   ❏ Sometimes Applies   ❏ Does Not Apply

1. **Which of the above quotes is closest to your own idea of acceptance? Why?**

   _____
   _____
   _____

2. **Which presents the greatest challenge to you? Why?**

   _____
   _____
   _____

Please do not duplicate.

Personal Notes

Personal Notes

---

[1] Russell Lynes, U.S. editor, critic, *The Readers Digest* (Pleasantville, NY: December 1954)
[2] John Cook, *Positive, Motivational, Life-Affirming & Inspirational Quotations* (Newington, CT: Rebicon Press, Inc., 1994)
[3] John Cook, *Positive, Motivational, Life-Affirming & Inspirational Quotations* (Newington, CT: Rebicon Press, Inc., 1994)
[4] H. Jackson Brown, Jr., *A Father's Book of Wisdom* (Nashville: Rutledge Hill Press, 1988)
[5] Herbert v. Prochnow, *Speaker's & Toastmaster's Handbook* (Rocklin, CA: Primas Publishing, 1993)
[6] Ibid
[7] Ibid
[8] Ibid

Please do not duplicate.

Other EZ Lesson Plans

The EZ Lesson Plan was designed with the facilitator in mind. This new format gives you the flexibility as a teacher to use the video as the visual and then refer to the facilitator's guide for the questions....and even better, the answers. It is designed for a four-week study, communicated by our top authors and it is totally self contained. **Each EZ Lesson Plan requires the student's guides to be purchased separately as we have maintained a very low purchase price on the video resource.**

Please visit your local Christian bookstore to see the other titles we have available in the EZ Lesson Plan format. We have listed some of the titles and authors for your convenience:

The 10 Commandments of Dating **Ben Young and Dr. Samuel Adams**
AVAILABLE NOW

Are you tired of pouring time, energy, and money into relationships that start off great and end with heartache? If so, you need The 10 Commandments of Dating to give you the hard-hitting, black-and-white, practical guidelines that will address your questions and frustrations about dating. This guide will help you keep your head in the search for the desire of your heart.
EZ Lesson Plan ISBN: 0-7852-9619-0 **Student's Guide ISBN: 0-7852-9621-2**

Extreme Evil: Kids Killing Kids **Bob Larson**
AVAILABLE NOW

Kids are killing kids in public schools! Kids are killing their parents! What is causing all of this evil in our younger generation? Do we need prayer back in the schools...or do we need God to start in the home? Bob Larson gets us to the root of these evils and brings us some of the answers we are looking for in this new video assisted program.
EZ Lesson Plan ISBN: 0-7852-9701-4 **Student's Guide ISBN: 0-7852-9702-2**

Life Is Tough, but God Is Faithful **Sheila Walsh**
AVAILABLE NOW

Sheila takes a look at eight crucial turning points that can help you rediscover God's love and forgiveness. Showing how the choices you make affect your life, she offers insights from the book of Job, from her own life, and from the lives of people whose simple but determined faith helped them become shining lights in a dark world.
EZ Lesson Plan ISBN: 0-7852-9618-2 **Student's Guide ISBN: 0-7852-9620-4**

Why I Believe **D. James Kennedy**
AVAILABLE NOW

In this video, Dr. D. James Kennedy offers intelligent, informed responses to frequently heard objections to the Christian faith. By dealing with topics such as the Bible, Creation, the Resurrection and the return of Christ, Why I Believe provides a solid foundation for Christians to clarify their own thinking while becoming more articulate in the defense of their faith.
EZ Lesson Plan ISBN: 0-7852-8770-9 **Student's Guide ISBN: 0-7852-8769-5**

The Lord's Prayer   **Jack Hayford**
AVAILABLE NOW

Why do we say "Thy Kingdom come?" What does "Hallowed be Thy Name" mean? Do we really practice "Forgive us our debts as we forgive our debtors?" Pastor Jack Hayford walks you through verse by verse and then applies his great scripture to our personal lives. This study will put "meaning to the words" you have just been saying for years.
EZ Lesson Plan ISBN: 0-7852-9442-2   **Student's Guide ISBN: 0-7852-9609-3**

How To Pray   **Ronnie Floyd**
AVAILABLE NOW

Whether you are a rookie in prayer or a seasoned prayer warrior, this video kit will meet you where you are and take you to another level in your prayer life. You may have been raised in a Christian home where prayer was a normal, daily exercise. You may have attended church all of your life, where the prayers of the people and the minister were as common as the hymns that still ring in your ears. Yet such experiences do not guarantee that you know how to pray. With simple, yet profound prose, Dr. Floyd declares, "prayer occurs when you depend on God, prayerlessness occurs when you depend on yourself."
EZ Lesson Plan ISBN: 0-8499-8790-3   **Student's Guide ISBN: 0-8499-8793-8**

Healing Prayer   **Reginald Cherry, M.D.**
AVAILABLE NOW

"Prayer is the divine key that unlocks God's pathway to healing in both the natural and supernatural realms of life." In Healing Prayer, he explores the connection between faith and healing, the Bible and medicine. Cherry blends the latest research, true stories, and biblical principles to show that spirit-directed prayers can bring healing for disease.
EZ Lesson Plan ISBN: 0-7852-9666-2   **Student's Guide ISBN: 0-7852-9667-0**

Jesus and The Terminator   **Jack Hayford**
AVAILABLE NOW

From the **E-Quake** Series comes the EZ Lesson Plan that is the focal point of the Book of Revelation. Pastor Hayford sets the stage for the fight against the Evil One when the end of time comes upon us. There is no greater force than that of Jesus and now viewers will see Him become triumphant again in this battle that is evident.
EZ Lesson Plan ISBN: 0-7852-9601-8   **Student's Guide ISBN: 0-7852-9658-1**

The Law of Process   **John C. Maxwell**
AVAILABLE NOW

Leadership develops daily, not in a day. This law, taken from **The Twenty One Irrefutable Laws of Leadership** is the first of the series to be placed into an individual study. Take each opportunity as it comes along and find the answer in a way only strong leaders would do it….by processing it. John explains how and why "Champions don't become champions in the ring…they are merely recognized there."
EZ Lesson Plan ISBN: 0-7852-9671-9   **Student's Guide ISBN: 0-7852-9672-7**

Forgiveness
AVAILABLE NOW
John MacArthur

In this three-session EZ Lesson Plan, noted biblical scholar John MacArthur provides an insightful look at forgiveness. MacArthur not only reminds us that we are called to grant forgiveness to those who sin against us, but he also teaches the importance of learning to accept the forgiveness of others.
EZ Lesson Plan ISBN: 0-8499-8808-X   **Student's Guide ISBN: 0-8499-8809-8**

Andy Griffith Volume 1 Bible Study Series
AVAILABLE NOW
Systems Media, Inc.

For generations, stories have been used to teach universal truths. In keeping with this time-honored tradition, the new three-volume Andy Griffith Bible Study Series has been developed, which uses the classic stories of Mayberry to illustrate biblical truths. In *Honesty*, the first volume of the series, learn from Andy, Opie, and the gang as they struggle with, and learn from, everyday life situations.
EZ Lesson Plan ISBN: 0-8499-8815-2   **Student's Guide ISBN: 0-8499-8816-0**

Created To Be God's Friend
AVAILABLE NOW
Henry Blackaby

Henry Blackaby being born a man of God, living his life as a man of God, teaches us how all of us are created equal in being God's friend. No Christian need live without a keen sense of purpose, and no believer need give up on finding daily closeness with God.
EZ Lesson Plan ISBN: 0-7852-9718-9   **Student's Guide ISBN: 0-7852-9719-7**

The Murder of Jesus
AVAILABLE NOW
John MacArthur

To many, the story of Christ's crucifixion has become so familiar that is has lost its ability to shock, outrage or stir any great emotion. In *The Murder of Jesus*, John MacArthur presents this pivotal moment in the life of Jesus in a way that forces the viewers to witness this event in all its power. The passion of Christ is examined chronoligically through the lens of the New Testament with special attention given to Jesus' words on the cross, the miracles that attended the crucifixion, and the significance of Christ's atoning work.
EZ Lesson Plan ISBN: 0-8499-8796-2   **Student's Guide ISBN: 0-8499-8797-0**

Fresh Brewed Life
AVAILABLE NOW
Nicole Johnson

God is calling us to wake up, to shout an enthusiastic "Yes" to life, just as we say "Yes" to our first cup of coffee each morning. Nothing would please Him more than for us to live fresh-brewed lives steeped with His love, filling the world with the marvelous aroma of Christ. The EZ Lesson Plan will provide humor, vignettes, and in depth study to small groups all over on this topic.
EZ Lesson Plan ISBN: 0-7852-9723-5   **Student's Guide ISBN: 0-7852-9724-3**

The Law of Respect　　　　　　　　　　　　　　　　**John C. Maxwell**
AVAILABLE NOW

We are taught from our parents to respect others. Our business practices are to be ones of respecting others ideas, thoughts and mainly their motivations. We tend to get caught up in the daily routines, but if we do not respect those around us and the ones we work with, our success will be held at a low ebb. John Maxwell is a leader's leader.
EZ Lesson Plan ISBN: 0-7852-9756-1　　　　　　　　**Student's Guide ISBN: 0-7852-9757-X**

Becoming A Woman of Grace　　　　　　　　　　　**Cynthia Heald**
AVAILABLE NOW

This is a newly formatted product built around a message that only Cynthia Heald could deliver to us. Women have proven to be the stronger of the sexes in prayer, empathy and faith. Cynthia leads this women's group study on how a woman can become A Woman of Grace through prayer, obedience to God and other practices of their lives. This EZ Lesson Plan will bring the components of this publishing product to one, self-contained format ready to start small groups.
EZ Lesson Plan ISBN: 0-7852-9706-5　　　　　　　　**Student's Guide ISBN: 0-7852-9707-3**

Andy Griffith Volume 2 Bible Study Series　　　　　**Systems Media**
AVAILABLE NOW

In the Andy Griffith Volume 2 Bible Study Series you will see four great studies: First lesson: "A Wife for Andy" teaches us about integrity in looking for a spouse, as well as in handling friends a bit over eager to see their plans to help us succeed-even if it kills us! Second lesson: "High Noon in Mayberry" illustrates the futility of worry, both in mind and in action. When Andy decides not to assume the worst, he is able to relax and enjoy the true intent of his former enemy's visit. Not so, for the posse outside his door! Third lesson: "Barney's First Car" is a roller-coaster ride of elation, dejection, amazement, and deception as Barney's friends loyally support him through his crisis. Fourth lesson: "The Great Filling Station Robbery" demonstrates the damage we can do to other's reputations when our perceptions do not keep pace with their growth.
EZ Lesson Plan ISBN: 0-8499-8832-2　　　　　　　　**Student's Guide ISBN: 0-8499-8833-0**

The Ten Commandments　　　　　　　　　　　　　**Jack Hayford**
AVAILABLE NOW

We are all taught the Ten Commandments early in our Christian walk. Dr. Jack Hayford now takes us one step farther and teaches us each of these commandments by a video-assisted method. Dr. Hayford teaches us to honor our fathers and our mothers by first teaching us to honor our Lord. All ten commandments will be taught over a four-session study. Studies with the comprehensive study material sold separately.
EZ Lesson Plan ISBN: 0-7852-9771-5　　　　　　　　**Student's Guide ISBN: 0-7852-9772-3**